Off to Grandma's House

Written by Mary Patton

Illustrated by Michelle Barnes

📖 ScottForesman

A Division of HarperCollins*Publishers*

In the car.

Bippity-bop, bippity-bop,
off to Grandma's house.

Down the driveway.

Bippity-bop, bippity-bop,
off to Grandma's house.

Around the curve.

Bippity-bop, bippity-bop,
off to Grandma's house.

Through the tunnel.

Bippity-bop, bippity-bop,
off to Grandma's house.

Down the highway.

Bippity-bop, bippity-bop,
off to Grandma's house.

Under the bridge.

Bippity-bop, bippity-bop,
off to Grandma's house.

14

Over the rock.
SSSSsssss.

Flippity-flop, flippity-flop,
on the driveway at Grandma's
house.